D0690089

THE AMERICAN FIREHOUSE COOKBOOK

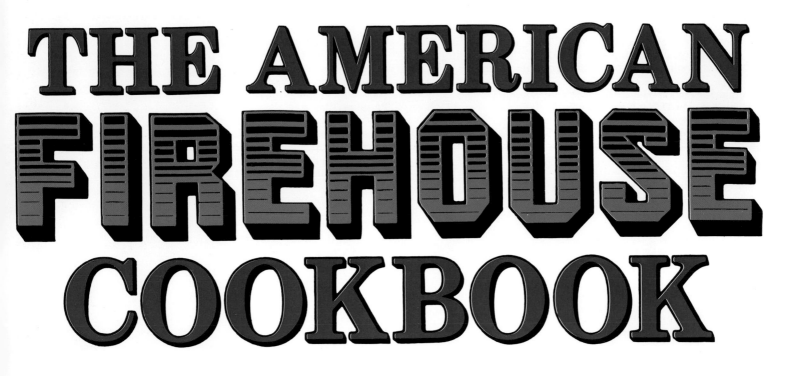

THE AMERICAN FIREHOUSE COOKBOOK

Edited by
Dave Corrigan

Crescent Books
New York/Avenel, New Jersey

Copyright © 1992 Brompton Books Corporation

All rights reserved. No part of this publication may be reproduced, stored in a retrieval system or transmitted in any form by any means, electronic, mechanical, photocopying or otherwise, without first obtaining written permission of the copyright owner.

This 1992 edition published by Crescent Books, distributed by Outlet Book Company, Inc., a Random House Company, 40 Engelhard Avenue, Avenel, New Jersey 07001.

Produced by
Brompton Books Corporation
15 Sherwood Place,
Greenwich, CT 06830

ISBN 0-517-06984-9

8 7 6 5 4 3 2 1

Printed and bound in Hong Kong

Designed by Ruth DeJauregui

Page 2: *Cranberry-Glazed Ham, recipe on page 70.*

Acknowledgments
I wish to acknowledge the following for their kind cooperation: Judith Koch, Julie Hamilton, Wilson Ray, the Fairfield Department of Public Safety, the San Francisco Fire Department, the Washington Apple Commission and the California Table Grape Commission. Special thanks to my friend and colleague, Lynne Piade, for her unfailing support during all stages of work.

Photo credits
Alaska Seafood Marketing Institute 48-56
Almond Board of California 72, 73
American Graphic Systems Archives 1
American Lamb Council 58, 60, 62-63
California Artichoke Advisory Board 40, 76
California Beef Council 10, 14, 21, 26
California Fig Advisory Board 34-35
California Olive Industry 32, 57, 75, 77-79
California Poultry Industry Federation 42, 43, 45, 46
California Tree Fruit Agreement, Sacramento 19, 37
Cling Peach Advisory Board 39, 74
© RE DeJauregui 6-9
Frozen Vegetable Council 38, 41
Idaho Bean Commission 70
National Honey Board 47
National Live Stock and Meat Board 2, 11, 13, 15-18, 20, 22-25, 27-31, 33, 59, 61, 64-69, 71
Washington State Potato Commission 36

Contents

Introduction

Above: *Wilson Ray of the Fairfield Department of Public Safety cleans the firehouse grill after a meal.*

For all firefighters, the dinner hour is the highlight of the day. Supper is the time when we can show off our skills in the kitchen. It's a tradition that stations eat lunch and dinner together. I for one heartily enjoyed the few quiet meals eaten with my company that weren't interrupted by the sound of the alarm. If the alarm sounded we'd turn off the stove and leave the table with everything on it. After the emergency had passed we would return to the station and reheat whatever was left of our dinner.

Fighting fires is hard work and when it comes to meals we want something satisfying. *The American Firehouse Cookbook* brings you the recipes firefighters like to cook and like to eat. Usually this means something that is simple, hearty and delicious, like Pork and Beans, Sausage with Sweet Potatoes and Apples, Chili, Corned Beef, Pot Roast and Lamb Chops. Some of us learned how to cook to keep from starving or as an economical alternative to dining out. For others, our parents and grandparents majored in sturdy cuisine and we'd like to think that our ability in the kitchen was passed on to us from them. Independent of our backgrounds we can all agree with this adage: 'Use only the freshest ingredients and it's hard to go wrong.'

It seems that everyone today is trying to watch their weight and cut down on cholesterol. Firefighters are no exception. A nationwide program of health awareness has found fire companies out together on a morning jog through the park. In the kitchen, companies are preparing more fresh vegetables, leaner cuts of meat, chicken and seafood. Included here are some delicious recipes that are high in nutritional value and low in calories, fat, sodium and cholesterol.

Each member of the firehouse takes a turn as chef, and we take pride in our cooking. One could say that we're inspired to outdo ourselves because we know that our audience is literally a captive one and truly appreciative. Beef is a favorite among firefighters. While this cookbook is abundant in

meat recipes, it reflects the taste and thrift of firefighters. Not only do we like hearty, one-pot meals that get tastier as they simmer over a low flame, but we have to pay for our own meals. Keeping an eye on the budget has motivated many firefighters to prepare innovative recipes using the lesser cuts of meat, some of which are included here. Served with noodles, over rice, in soup, in sauce and with vegetables, beef satisfies the heartiest appetites and its subtle flavor appeases even the most discriminating epicures.

Chicken, turkey and duck make highly nutritious, low-calorie meals that are delicious hot or cold. Poultry can be baked, fried or grilled, and used in casseroles, fondues, salads and soups. Bought fresh from your butcher it can be quickly cooked and offers endless variety. It is usually cheaper to buy a whole bird and cut it up at home to suit the recipe, but it is a bit of a chore, and for some the saving is not worth the effort. Luckily, chicken and turkey parts are available packaged in a variety of combinations. Chicken and turkey breasts that have been skinned and filleted are an especially popular choice because of the time they save.

Fish and seafood have a broad appeal and can be baked, broiled, barbecued, steamed, poached, fried, boiled, stewed and sautéed. Both can be served hot or cold, as an appetizer or main dish, in soup, salad, stir-fry or pasta. Not everyone is lucky enough to go out on a quiet lake or wade into a mountain stream and hook something for supper. Perhaps once or twice a month a group of us will go fishing or cast a line off the end of the pier. Most of us, however, buy fish at the market, where a lot of the time it's been cleaned, cut up, prepared and packaged for our convenience.

Here are some hints to choosing fresh whole fish. Look for fish with clear, full eyes, slightly bulging, not cloudy or sunken-looking. The gills should be bright red, not pinkish or dark brown. Scales and skin should be unbruised,

Above: *Captain Frank Cardinale of the San Francisco Fire Department pauses a moment in front of the station.*

Above, left: *Some of the firehouse gang help themselves to salad before dinner has officially begun.*

8

attached, moist and shiny but never slimy. The flesh should be firm to the touch and leave no indentation. Fresh fish has a mild, pleasant, briny odor, not sour.

Salmon, a favorite catch, has many health benefits and is a good alternative to meals which are high in saturated fats and calories. It offers large quantities of protein and significant amounts of vitamins and minerals as well.

Some of our firefighters like to cook ethnic food, so you'll find Greek, Creole, Mexican, Irish and Chinese dishes right next to the ribs, stews, chowders and chops.

The recipes in this cookbook have been tested and scaled down to serve four to six persons. To help keep things simple, preparation and cooking times are clearly indicated above each easy-to-follow recipe. Guides to choosing fresh ingredients and useful cooking tips are included too. I hope you'll enjoy the recipes in this cookbook as much as I have. And remember, if you're cooking and eating like American firefighters at your house, the cook doesn't have to do the dishes.

Right: *When the alarm sounds, these friendly guys become all business as they swing into action.*

Below: *A place for every thing and everything in its place.*

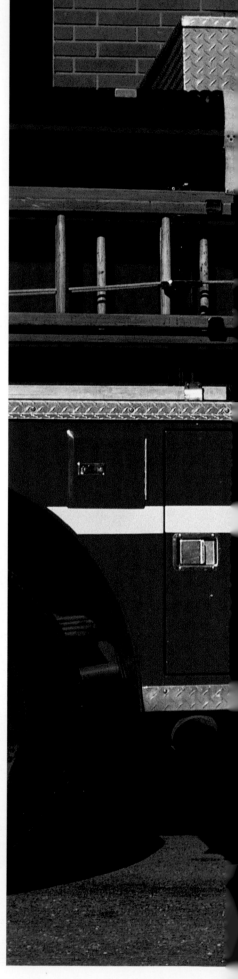

Beef Tenderloin Roast

Preparation time: 2 minutes
Cooking time: 45 to 60 minutes

4- to 6-pound (1.8 to 2.7 *kg*) beef tenderloin (fillet) roast

Heat oven to 425°F (220°C). Place roast on rack in shallow roasting pan. Insert meat thermometer in roast, placing bulb or tip in the center of the largest muscle. Do not add water and do not cover the roasting pan. Cook roast 45 to 60 minutes or until thermometer reads 135°F (60°C). Allow roast to 'rest' 15 to 20 minutes before carving. The roast will continue to cook during this time. Serve beef tenderloin rare since it is a particularly tender and juicy cut of beef. An average tenderloin roast serves 10 to 12 people.

Holiday Beef Steaks with Vegetable Sauté and Hot Mustard Sauce

Preparation time: 15 minutes
Cooking time: 15 minutes

Boneless beef top loin steaks, cut 1-inch (3 *cm*) thick
½ cup (15 *g*) plain yogurt
1 teaspoon (5 *g*) cornstarch (cornflour)
¼ cup (60 *ml*) condensed beef broth
2 teaspoons (10 *g*) coarse-grained mustard
1 teaspoon (5 *g*) prepared grated horseradish
1 teaspoon (5 *g*) Dijon-style mustard
¼ teaspoon (1 *g*) sugar
½ teaspoon (2 *g*) lemon-pepper
1 package (16 ounces/450 *g*) frozen whole green beans
1 cup (225 *g*) quartered large mushrooms
1 tablespoon (15 *g*) butter
¼ cup (60 *ml*) water

Place yogurt and cornstarch in a medium-sized saucepan and stir until blended. Stir in beef broth, coarse-grained mustard, horseradish, Dijon-style mustard and sugar; reserve. Press an equal amount of lemon-pepper into surface of boneless beef loin steaks. Place steaks on rack in broiler pan so surface of steaks is three to four inches from heat. Broil steaks about 15 minutes for rare; 20 minutes for medium, turning once.

Meanwhile, cook beans and mushrooms in butter in large frying pan over medium heat for six minutes, stirring occasionally. Add water, cover and continue cooking six to eight minutes, stirring occasionally until beans are tender. Cook reserved sauce over medium-low heat for five minutes, stirring until sauce is slightly thickened. Serve steaks and vegetables with sauce. Makes six servings of vegetables and sauce.

Note: A boneless beef top loin steak will yield four, three-ounce (85 *g*) cooked servings per pound (450 *g*) (nine, 85-*g* cooked servings per kilogram).

Rotisserie Beef Tip Roast

Preparation time: 5 minutes
Cooking time: 1 hour 30 minutes to 4 hours

3 to 8 pound (1.35 to 3.6 *kg*) beef tip roast

Insert rotisserie rod lengthwise through center of beef tip roast. Balance roast and tighten spit forks so roast turns only with rod. Insert meat thermometer (at an angle so it will clear the cooking unit) so the tip is centered in the roast and does not rest in fat or on the rod. Place on rotisserie and roast over low to medium coals,* using indirect heat, to desired degree of doneness; 140°F (60°C) for rare; 160°F (70°C) for medium. Allow 30 to 35 minutes per pound (500 *g*) for a roast weighing three to five pounds (1.35 to 2.25 *kg*); 25 minutes to 30 minutes per pound (500 *g*) for a roast weighing five to eight pounds (2.25 to 3.6 *kg*). Serve with *Summer Pasta Salad*.

*Test about four inches (10 *cm*) above coals for low to medium with four- to five-second hand count.

Note: A beef tip roast will yield four, three-ounce cooked servings per pound (nine, 85 *g* cooked servings per *kg*).

Note: Roast may also be cooked in a covered cooker, using indirect heat. Prepare coals as usual, and allow 25 to 30 minutes per pound (500 *g*) for a roast weighing three to five pounds (1.35 to 2.25 *kg*); 20 to 25 minutes per pound (500 *g*) for a roast weighing five to eight pounds (2.25 to 3.6 *kg*).

Summer Pasta Salad
(pictured at right, behind roast)

Preparation time: 5 minutes
Cooking time: 12 to 20 minutes

1½ cups (340 *g*) pasta shells
¼ cup (60 *ml*) Italian dressing
1 tablespoon (15 *g*) coarsely grated Parmesan cheese
1 tablespoon (15 *g*) grated onion
2 teaspoons (10 *g*) chopped fresh basil
¾ teaspoon (7 *g*) salt
1 pinch white pepper
1½ cups (340 *g*) fresh or frozen peas, cooked
1 small tomato seeded and chopped

Cook pasta according to package directions. Cool. Combine Italian dressing, Parmesan cheese, onion, basil, salt and pepper. Place pasta shells, peas and tomato in medium-sized bowl; add Italian dressing mixture, stirring lightly to coat. Cover tightly and refrigerate one to two hours. Makes six servings.

Standing Beef Rib Roast

Preparation time: 10 minutes
Cooking time: 1 hour 45 minutes to 4 hours 15 minutes

4- to 6-pound (1.8 to 2.7 *kg*) beef standing rib roast

Place roast, fat side up, in open shallow roasting pan. Do not add water. Do not cover. Insert meat thermometer so bulb is centered in the thickest part of the roast. Roast in a 325°F (160°C) oven. The meat thermometer will register 140°F (60°C) for rare; 160°F (70°C) for medium; and 170°F (75°C) for well done. Allow 26 to 32 minutes per pound/450 *g* for rare, 34 to 38 minutes per pound/450 *g* for medium and 40 to 42 minutes per pound/450 *g* for well done.* Roasts usually continue to cook after removal from the oven. It is best to remove them when the thermometer registers 5°F/3°C below the temperature of desired doneness.

For easier carving, allow the roast to 'rest' in a warm place 15 to 20 minutes before carving. Makes eight to twelve servings.

*Note: For a 6- to 8-pound (2.7 to 3.6 *kg*) roast, allow 23 to 25 minutes per pound/450 *g* for rare, 27 to 30 minutes per pound/450 *g* for medium, and 32 and 35 minutes per pound/450 *g* for well done.

Light Braised Beef with Steamed Vegetables

Preparation time: 30 minutes
Cooking time: 2 hours 30 minutes

3 to 3½-pound (1.6 *kg*) boneless beef chuck arm
    pot roast
1 clove garlic
1 teaspoon (5 *g*) each salt, dried rosemary and
    thyme leaves
½ teaspoon (2 *g*) cracked black pepper
1 tablespoon (15 *ml*) oil
2 carrots, finely chopped
1 medium onion, finely chopped
1 rib celery, finely chopped
3 sprigs fresh parsley, minced
½ cup plus 2 tablespoons (150 *ml*) water, divided
¼ cup (60 *ml*) dry red wine
2 tablespoons (30 *g*) cornstarch
8 ounces (225 *g*) *each* carrots, Brussels sprouts and
    cauliflower florets

Mash garlic with French knife; combine with salt, rosemary, thyme and pepper to form a paste. Rub surface of beef chuck arm pot roast with garlic mixture. Brown pot roast in oil in a Dutch oven over medium-high heat. Remove and reserve. Quickly cook and stir carrots, onion, celery and parsley in same pan over medium-high heat until tender-crisp. Pour off drippings. Return pot roast to Dutch oven. Add ½ cup (120 *ml*) water and the wine, cover tightly and cook slowly 2 to 2½ hours or until beef is tender. Remove roast to warm platter. Strain cooking liquid; skim and discard fat. Combine cornstarch with remaining water, add to 2 cups (475 *ml*) cooking liquid and bring to a boil. Boil one minute, stirring constantly. Meanwhile, steam carrots, Brussels sprouts and cauliflower 12 to 15 minutes or until tender. Serve gravy and vegetables with pot roast.

Note: A boneless beef chuck arm pot roast will yield two to three, three-ounce (85 *g*) cooked servings per pound (450 *g*).

Editor's Note: Here are five simple tricks to making a good pot roast: First trim away any excess fat. For a rich, brown color, coat the roast on all sides with all-purpose flour. Slowly brown the roast in hot shortening, cooking oil or drippings from the melted fat trimmings. Add beef broth, tomato juice or water and the seasonings. Cover tightly and cook over low heat in a Dutch oven, or in a 325°F (160°C) oven, or in an electric frying pan set at 220°F (105°C).

Quick Beef Steaks with Corn Relish

Preparation time: 10 minutes
Cooking time: 10 minutes

1 pound (450 g) boneless beef chuck top blade
   steaks, cut ½-inch (12 mm) thick
1 teaspoon oil (5 ml)
½ red bell pepper, cut into ½-inch (12 mm) pieces
1 can (8¾ ounces/250 g) whole kernel corn,
   undrained

1 tablespoon (15 ml) white wine vinegar
1 pinch ground red pepper
¼ teaspoon (1 g) garlic salt
¼ cup (30 g) sliced scallions (spring onions)

Trim excess fat from beef top blade steaks; reserve. Cook and stir red pepper in oil in large non-stick frying pan over medium heat three minutes. Stir in corn, vinegar and pepper and continue cooking, uncovered, two to three minutes or until liquid is slightly reduced. Remove from frying pan and keep warm. Heat frying pan over medium-high heat until hot. Panbroil steaks three minutes, turning once. Season with garlic salt. Add corn mixture and onions to frying pan. Cook one minute or until heated through. Makes four servings.

Corned Beef Dinner

Preparation time: 6 minutes
Cooking time: 2½ to 3½ hours

2½ to 3 pounds (1 to 1.35 *kg*) corned beef brisket
12 whole peppercorns
1 bay leaf
   Water
6 small red potatoes, pared

¾ cup (170 *g*) celery, cut into 1-inch (3 *cm*) pieces
1 medium onion, cut into wedges
1 small cabbage head, cut into six wedges
½ cup (60 *g*) red pepper strips
1 tablespoon (15 *g*) snipped parsley

Place corned beef brisket, peppercorns, and bay leaf in Dutch oven; add water to cover. Cover tightly and simmer 2½ to 3½ hours or until meat is tender. Forty minutes before brisket is done, add potatoes and continue cooking, covered, 15 minutes. Add celery and onion and continue cooking three to five minutes. Place cabbage wedges over vegetables, and red pepper over cabbage. Cover tightly and continue cooking 17 to 20 minutes or until cabbage is done. Sprinkle with parsley. Carve meat diagonally across the grain into thin slices and serve with vegetables.

Hot and Spicy Beef Ribs

Preparation time: 12 to 15 minutes
Cooking time: 2 hours 10 minutes

7 pounds (3.15 *kg*) beef back ribs
¾ cup (180 *ml*) water, divided
1 cup (240 *ml*) catsup
2 tablespoons (30 *ml*) lemon juice
1 teaspoon (5 *ml*) ground cinnamon
1 teaspoon (5 *ml*) hot pepper sauce
½ to 1 teaspoon (2 to 5 *ml*) crushed red pepper pods

Place each slab of ribs, meat side down, in center of a double-thick rectangle of heavy duty aluminum foil that is twice the length of the slab plus eight inches (20 *cm*). Sprinkle 2 tablespoons (30 *ml*) water over rib bones. To form packets, bring two opposite sides of foil together over top of ribs. Fold edges over three or four times, pressing crease in sides of foil together over top of ribs. Fold edges over three or four times toward package, pressing tightly to seal. Repeat procedure on other end. Place packets on grill directly over low to medium coals.* Place cover on cooker and cook 1½ hours, turning packets over every ½ hour.

Meanwhile, combine catsup, remaining ½ cup (120 *ml*) water, lemon juice, cinnamon, hot pepper sauce and crushed red pepper in a small saucepan. Bring to a boil, reduce heat and cook slowly 10 to 12 minutes. Remove ribs from foil packets. Place on grill over medium coals* and broil 30 to 40 minutes, turning and brushing with sauce occasionally. Serve remaining sauce with ribs. Makes eight to ten servings.

*Test about four inches (10 *cm*) above coals for low to medium with a four- to five-second hand count.

Note: Ribs may also be cooked on an open brazier. Increase cooking time in packets 30 minutes.

Plum Blossom Barbecue Sauce and Glaze

Preparation time: 12 minutes
Cooking time: 4 minutes

¼ cup (30 *g*) finely chopped onion
1½ tablespoons (20 *g*) grated fresh ginger
1 clove garlic, minced
1 tablespoon (15 *ml*) vegetable oil
½ cup (120 *ml*) prune juice
¼ cup (60 *ml*) cider vinegar
6 tablespoons (85 *g*) sweet orange marmalade
1 teaspoon (5 *g*) crushed red pepper
¼ teaspoon (1 *g*) *each* salt and pepper
1 tablespoon (15 *g*) cornstarch (cornflour)
2 tablespoons (30 *ml*) water

In saucepan, sauté onions, ginger and garlic in oil until lightly browned. Stir in prune juice, vinegar, marmalade, crushed red pepper, salt and pepper. Bring to a boil, stirring; boil 1 minute. Dissolve cornstarch in water; stir in. Cook and stir until thickened and clear. Store in covered container in refrigerator. Use as a basting sauce and glaze for barbecued or broiled meats. Serve additional sauce on the side for dipping. Makes about 1 ½ cups (375 *ml*).

Grilled Sirloin Steak with Red Onion Kabobs

Preparation time: 10 minutes
Marinating time: 30 minutes
Cooking time: 16 to 20 minutes

1¼ pounds (575 g) boneless beef sirloin (rump) steak, cut 1 inch (3 cm) thick
¼ cup (60 ml) red wine vinegar
3 tablespoons (45 ml) olive oil
2 teaspoons (9 g) dried oregano leaves, divided

1 teaspoon (5 ml) honey
¾ teaspoon (3 g) cracked black pepper, divided
½ teaspoon (2 g) *each* dry mustard and salt
1 medium red onion, cut into 8 wedges through core

Combine vinegar, oil, 1½ teaspoons (7 g) oregano, honey, ¼ teaspoon (1 g) pepper, mustard and salt. Place onions in a plastic bag; add marinade, turning to coat. Close bag securely and marinate while coals are being prepared.

Meanwhile, soak eight, six-inch (15 cm) bamboo skewers in water 10 minutes. Combine remaining oregano and black pepper. Press herb mixture evenly into both sides of beef sirloin (rump) steak. Remove onions from marinade; reserve marinade. Skewer onion wedges in two places through all layers, placing two wedges on skewers; repeat three times.

Place steak and kabobs on grill over medium coals,* turning steaks and onions once. Brush with reserved marinade occasionally. Broil about 16 minutes for rare; 20 minutes for medium. Makes four servings.

*Test about four inches (10 cm) above coals for medium with a five-second hand count.

Grilled Beef Strips

Preparation time: 7 minutes
Marinating time: 8 hours
Cooking time: 10 to 15 minutes

1½ pounds (675 g) beef skirt steak, flank steak or
   rump steak
½ cup (120 ml) red wine vinegar
½ cup (120 ml) lemon juice
¼ cup (60 ml) vegetable oil
4 large cloves garlic, crushed
1 large onion, sliced
1 can (7 ounces/200 g) whole green chilies, sliced
   lengthwise

1 tablespoon (15 ml) Worcestershire sauce
1 teaspoon (5 g) dried oregano
½ teaspoon (3 g) black pepper
  Salt to taste
1 dozen flour tortillas
1 avocado, sliced
1 cup (225 g) sour cream

Place steak in large glass baking dish. Mix next 10 ingredients; pour over steak. Cover and refrigerate at least eight hours, no longer than 48 hours. Remove onions from marinade and discard marinade. Wrap onions in aluminum foil. Wrap tortillas in foil. Place on grill next to steak.

Grill steak four inches (10 cm) over medium-hot coals five minutes on each side for rare, longer if desired. To serve, cut steak against the grain into thin slices. For each serving, place about two slices steak and some onions on each tortilla. Serve with avocado and sour cream. Makes six servings.

22

Broiled Rib Eye Steaks

Preparation time: 5 minutes
Cooking time: 12 to 30 minutes

Beef rib eye steaks, cut 1 to 1½ inches (2.5 to 4 *cm*)
   thick
Salt and pepper

Place beef rib eye steaks on grill over medium coals,*
turning once. Steaks cut 1 inch (3 *cm*) thick require 12 to 15
minutes for rare; 18 to 20 minutes for medium. Steaks cut
1½ inches (4 *cm*) thick require 23 to 25 minutes for rare; 28
to 30 minutes for medium. Season with salt and pepper.

*Test about four inches (10 *cm*) above coals for medium
with a four-second hand count.

Fruit Salad with Two Dressings
(not pictured)

Preparation time: 5 minutes

1 red delicious apple, cored and sliced
1 orange, peeled, sliced and quartered
2 cups (250 *g*) green grapes, seeded if necessary
½ cup (200 *g*) pineapple chunks
   Sweet Lemon Vinaigrette or *Creamy Yogurt Dressing*
   Lettuce leaves (optional)

Combine fruits. Coat salad with your choice of dressing.
The vinaigrette-coated salad may be served immediately.
Refrigerate the creamy-coated salad at least one hour.
Arrange fruit salad in lettuce-lined bowl or individual cups
if desired. Makes four to six servings.

Sweet Lemon Vinaigrette

2 tablespoons (30 *ml*) lemon juice
1 tablespoon (15 *ml*) *each* vegetable oil and sugar
1 dash *each* salt and cayenne pepper

Combine ingredients in a jar with a tight lid. Shake vigor-
ously and pour over fruit salad.

Creamy Yogurt Dressing

⅓ cup (75 *g*) orange or lemon-flavored yogurt
¼ cup (25 *g*) broken walnuts

Add walnuts and yogurt to fruit mixture and stir gently to
coat.

Beef and Mushrooms in White Wine Sauce

Preparation time: 10 to 15 minutes
Cooking time: 4 hours 20 minutes

2½ pounds (1.15 *kg*) boneless beef chuck, cut into
    1-inch (3 *cm*) pieces
¼ pound (125 *g*) butter or margarine
¼ cup (60 *ml*) cognac, if desired
  4 carrots, quartered and cut into 2½-inch (6 *cm*)
    sticks
  3 carrots, grated
  2 onions, diced
  6 tablespoons (85 *g*) flour
  2 cloves garlic, finely sliced
  3 bay leaves
1½ teaspoons (7 *g*) *each* ground thyme and salt
  ¼ teaspoon (2 *g*) pepper
  2 cups (475 *ml*) white Chablis wine
  1 pound (450 *g*) fresh mushrooms, halved
16 to 20 small white onions (approximately 1 inch/3
    cm in diameter), peeled
    French bread, if desired

Brown boneless beef chuck in butter in heavy metal casserole dish or Dutch oven. If desired, heat cognac, ignite and pour over beef. Add carrot sticks, grated carrots, diced onion, flour, garlic, bay leaves, thyme, salt and pepper; mix lightly. Stir in wine. Cover and bake in a 375°F (190°C) moderately hot oven two hours, stirring every half hour. Add mushrooms and onions, cover and continue baking two hours, stirring occasionally. Adjust seasoning to taste. Remove bay leaves. Serve with French bread, if desired. Makes eight servings.

Note: Liquid should become a thick sauce. If sauce is too thin, adjust oven temperature to 400°F (205°C) during last 20 minutes of cooking time. If sauce is too thick, add water.

Broiled Beef Porterhouse and Vegetable Dinner

Preparation time: 5 minutes
Cooking time: 28 to 30 minutes

1 frozen beef porterhouse steak* (1 pound/500 *g*),
    cut 1-inch (3 *cm*) thick
1 medium yellow squash, cut in half lengthwise
1 small red bell pepper, cut into 8 wedges
2 tablespoons (30 *g*) grated Parmesan cheese
1 tablespoon (15 *ml*) olive oil
½ teaspoon (2 *g*) *each* dried Italian seasoning and salt
1 pinch pepper

When preparing a fresh steak, place frozen beef porterhouse steak on rack in broiler pan so surface of meat is four to five inches (10 to 12 *cm*) from the heat. Broil first side of steak 15 minutes. Meanwhile, combine cheese, oil and Italian seasoning; spread mixture on all sides of vegetables. Turn steak. Place squash (cut side up) and peppers around steak on broiler pan; turn and broil second side of steak 13 to 15 minutes to desired degree of doneness (rare or medium), turning vegetables over once during cooking. Season steak with salt and pepper. Makes two to three servings.

*When preparing a fresh steak, place fresh beef porterhouse steak on rack in broiler pan so surface of meat is three to four inches (8 to 10 *cm*) from heat. Broil steak 20 to 25 minutes to desired degree of doneness (rare or medium), turning steak over once during cooking. Add vegetables the last 15 minutes of cooking time, turning once.

Beef Steak with Artichokes

Preparation time: 15 minutes
Cooking time: 20 minutes

1 teaspoon (5 *ml*) vegetable oil
2 pounds (900 *g*) beef top sirloin steak
1 pound (500 *g*) fresh mushrooms, sliced
⅔ cup (160 *ml*) dry white wine
½ cup (120 *ml*) beef broth
2 packages (9 ounces/510 *g* each) frozen artichokes,
  defrosted
2 teaspoons (10 *g*) grated lemon peel
2 teaspoons (10 *g*) dried oregano leaves
2 teaspoons (10 *g*) dried thyme leaves
½ teaspoon (3 *g*) salt

Trim external fat from steak. Brush non-stick surface 12-inch (30 *cm*) frying pan with vegetable oil. Place steak in frying pan. Cook over medium heat, turning occasionally to brown the steak evenly on both sides. Cook eight to ten minutes total cooking time for rare, or until desired doneness. Remove from frying pan; keep warm in 200°F (95°C) oven.

Meanwhile, stir mushrooms into frying pan. Cook and stir over medium heat until mushrooms are coated with beef drippings. Stir in wine. Increase heat to high. Reduce wine by two-thirds. Stir in remaining ingredients; cover. Simmer until artichokes are crisp-tender, about three minutes. Makes three cups (750 *ml*) sauce. Cut steak into slices. Serve artichoke topping with steak. Makes eight servings.

Szechwan Beef Strips

Preparation time: 15 minutes
Cooking time: 5 minutes

2 boneless beef chuck top blade steaks cut ½ inch
  (1.25 *cm*) thick (8 to 10 ounces/150 to 175 *g*)
1 tablespoon (15 *ml*) *each* catsup, soy sauce and dry
  sherry
1 teaspoon *each* brown sugar (5 *g*), cornstarch
  (cornflour 5 *g*) and white vinegar (5 *ml*)
1 tablespoon (15 *ml*) plus 1 teaspoon (5 *ml*) oil
½ teaspoon (2 *g*) minced fresh ginger
1 clove garlic, minced
1 pinch to ¼ teaspoon (1 *g*) crushed red pepper pods
1 large carrot, cut into thin strips 2½ inches (5 *cm*)
  long
1 large stalk of celery, cut into thin strips 2½ inches
  (5 *cm*) long
2 scallions (spring onions) with tops, sliced
  Cooked rice, if desired

Partially freeze beef chuck top blade steaks to firm. Divide each steak into two pieces, following natural seam and removing connective tissue between pieces. Cut each piece across the grain into thin strips; reserve. Combine catsup, soy sauce, sherry, brown sugar, cornstarch and vinegar; reserve.

Heat 1 tablespoon (15 *ml*) oil in medium frying pan over medium-high heat. Add ginger, garlic and red pepper; cook and stir 30 seconds. Stir-fry beef in hot seasoned oil for one minute. Remove from pan; reserve. Heat remaining oil over medium heat. Add carrots and celery, cook and stir one minute. Add reserved beef and sauce to frying pan; continue to cook and stir one to two minutes or until sauce thickens. Stir in scallions. Serve immediately over cooked rice, if desired. Makes two servings.

Five-Way Chili

Preparation time: 15 minutes
Cooking time: 1 hour

1½ pounds (675 *g*) ground beef
 1 medium onion, finely chopped
 2 cloves garlic, minced
 2 tablespoons (30 *g*) chili powder
 1 tablespoon (15 *g*) unsweetened cocoa
 1 teaspoon (5 *g*) *each* dry mustard, ground cumin,
  paprika and salt
¼ teaspoon (1 *g*) *each* ground red and black pepper

 1 pinch *each* ground allspice, cardamom, cinnamon
  and cloves
 1 can (28 ounces/800 *g*) Italian plum tomatoes
 1 cup (250 *ml*) water
 8 ounces (225 *g*) vermicelli,* cooked
 1 can (15¼ ounces/425 *g*) red kidney beans, heated
 1 small onion, finely chopped
 4 ounces (115 *g*) Cheddar cheese, finely shredded

Cook ground beef with onion and garlic in a Dutch oven over medium-high heat until beef loses its pink color. Pour off drippings. Stir in chili powder, cocoa, dry mustard, cumin, paprika, salt, red and black pepper, allspice, cardamom, cinnamon, cloves, tomatoes and water. Bring to a boil; reduce heat and simmer, uncovered 45 minutes.

This recipe gets its name from the way it is served. Depending on the number of ingredients piled on top of each other, this famous chili can be served as Five-Way, Four-Way or Three-Way Chili. To assemble Five-Way Chili, layer the following ingredients on six individual plates: vermicelli, beans, chili mixture, onion and cheese. To serve Four-Way Chili, layer vermicelli, the chili mixture, onion and cheese; to serve Three-Way Chili layer vermicelli, chili mixture and cheese. Makes six servings.

*Thin spaghetti may be substituted for the vermicelli.

Mandarin Beef

Preparation time: 15 minutes
Marinating time: 30 minutes
Cooking time: 15 minutes

1 pound (450 g) beef flank steak (rump steak)
3 tablespoons (45 ml) light soy sauce, divided
2 tablespoons (30 ml) vegetable oil, divided
1 tablespoon (15 g) cornstarch (cornflour)
1 tablespoon (15 g) brown sugar, divided
¼ pound (115 g) green beans, cut into 2-inch (5 cm)
    diagonal pieces

1 package (10 ounces/275 g) frozen asparagus*
    defrosted and cut into 2-inch (5 cm) diagonal
    pieces
¼ pound (125 g) mushrooms, sliced
2 tablespoons (30 ml) dry sherry
6 scallions, cut into 2-inch (5 cm) slivers
½ teaspoon (2 ml) Oriental dark roasted sesame oil

Cut beef flank steak in half lengthwise. Cut steak across the grain into ⅛-inch (3 ml) thick strips. Combine 1 tablespoon (15 ml) soy sauce, 1 teaspoon (5 ml) oil, cornstarch and 1 teaspoon (5 ml) brown sugar; pour over beef strips and marinate 30 minutes.

Heat non-stick frying pan over medium heat; add remaining oil. Stir-fry green beans three to four minutes; add asparagus and mushrooms and cook two minutes. Remove vegetables; keep warm. Combine sherry, remaining soy sauce and sugar; reserve. Stir-fry beef (one-third at a time) two to three minutes; reserve.

Return beef, vegetables and sherry mixture to frying pan and heat through. Stir in scallions. Add sesame oil and stir. Serve immediately. Makes four servings.

*Twelve ounces (350 g) fresh asparagus may be substituted. Cut into 2-inch (5 cm) diagonal pieces; blanch two minutes before stir-frying.

Chunky Beef Chili

Preparation time: 30 to 40 minutes
Cooking time: 2 hours 15 minutes to 2 hours 30 minutes

2½ pounds (1.2 *kg*) boneless beef chuck, cut into
    ½-inch (12 *mm*) pieces
1 cup (125 *g*) coarsely chopped onion
1 green pepper, chopped
2 cloves garlic, minced
2 tablespoons (30 *ml*) cooking oil
1 teaspoon (5 *g*) salt
1 can (28 ounces/800 *g*) Italian plum tomatoes,
    broken up
1 cup (250 *ml*) water
1 can (6 ounces/170 *g*) tomato paste
3 tablespoons (40 *g*) chili powder
1 teaspoon (5 *g*) dried oregano leaves
½ teaspoon (2 *g*) crushed red pepper pods, if desired
1 can (15½ ounces/435 *g*) kidney beans, drained
    Condiments: dairy sour cream, shredded sharp
    Cheddar cheese, chopped onion and avocado
    chunks

Brown beef, onion, green pepper and garlic in oil in a
large frying pan or Dutch oven. Pour off drippings. Sprinkle
salt over beef. Add tomatoes, water, tomato paste, chili
powder, oregano and crushed red pepper, if desired. Cover
tightly and cook slowly 1½ hours or until beef is tender. Add
beans and continue cooking, uncovered, 20 to 30 minutes.
Garnish with sour cream, cheese, onion and avocado, as
desired. Makes two quarts (almost 2 *l*), approximately six to
eight servings.

Spicy Beef Stew

Preparation time: 10 minutes
Cooking time: 1 hour 40 minutes

1 pound (450 *g*) beef for stew, cut into 1 to 1¼-inch
    (3 to 7 *cm*) pieces
1 large onion, chopped
2 cloves garlic, minced
1 can (13¾ ounces/460 *ml*) single strength beef broth
½ cup (120 *ml*) picante sauce
1 large zucchini (courgette), cut into ¼-inch (5 *cm*)
    slices
1 large red or green bell pepper, cut into 1-inch (3 *cm*)
    pieces
2 teaspoons (10 *g*) cornstarch (cornflour)
2 tablespoons (30 *ml*) water

Brown beef for stew, with onion and garlic in a non-stick
Dutch oven over medium heat. Pour off drippings, if necessary. Add beef broth and picante sauce. Cover tightly and
cook slowly 1½ hours, stirring occasionally. Add zucchini
(courgette) and pepper pieces; continue cooking, covered,
10 minutes or until beef and vegetables are tender.
Combine cornstarch (cornflour) and water; add to stew.
Bring to a boil, cook and stir two minutes or until thickened.
Makes four servings.

Hearty Beef Tart

Preparation time: 15 minutes
Cooking time: 1 hour

¾ pound (325 g) ground beef
¾ cup (95 g) chopped onion
 1 can (15 ounces/435 g) tomato sauce
 1 cup (125 g) halved, pitted olives
 1 tablespoon (15 g) chili powder
¾ teaspoon (4 g) oregano, crumbled
½ teaspoon (2 ml) Tabasco sauce
  Masa Dough
 1 cup (125 g) Cheddar cheese cubes (½ inch/1 cm)
½ cup (25 g) grated Parmesan cheese

Sauté ground beef and onion in a large frying pan over high heat until browned, about four minutes. Remove from heat. Add 1 cup (200 g) tomato sauce, the olives, chili powder, oregano and Tabasco sauce and stir until well blended. Using spatula spread half of *Masa Dough* (1 cup/250 g) over bottom and sides of 9-inch (23-cm) pie plate. Spoon half of beef mixture into pan. Top with remaining tomato sauce and Cheddar cheese cubes. Cover with remaining beef. Pat remaining *Masa Dough* into four or five thin patties and lay on top of tart. Carefully spread patties over filling to completely enclose tart. Cover with foil and bake on bottom rack of 425°F (220°C) oven 45 minutes. Remove foil and continue baking 15 minutes or until top is golden. Sprinkle with Parmesan cheese before serving.

Masa Dough

Preparation time: 6 minutes

½ cup (115 g) margarine
1½ cups (225 g) masa harina (instant masa mix)
¾ teaspoon (4 g) instant chicken bouillon powder
¾ cup (180 ml) water

Beat margarine with electric mixer until fluffy. Blend in masa harina and chicken bouillon powder. Gradually beat in water. Then beat at high speed until well blended. Makes about 2 cups (500 g).

Microwave method: Combine crumbled-up beef and onion in a two-quart (2 l) rectangular glass baking dish. Microcook uncovered on high for nine minutes or until meat is no longer pink, stirring twice. Stir in 1 cup (200 g) tomato sauce, the chili powder, oregano, Tabasco sauce and olives. Make *Masa Dough*, assemble tart and bake in conventional oven as directed.

Creole-Style Beef Soup

Preparation time: 30 minutes
Cooking time: 2 hours 45 minutes

3 to 4 pounds (1.35 to 1.8 kg) beef shank cross cuts
4 cups (950 ml) water
1 can (28 ounces/800 g) crushed tomatoes
1 cup (170 g) sliced celery
1 large onion, chopped
2 cloves garlic, minced
2 beef bouillon cubes
½ teaspoon (2 g) salt
¼ teaspoon (1 g) *each* pepper and ground red pepper
2 cups (225 g) chopped cabbage
1 green bell pepper, chopped
¼ cup (60 ml) fresh lemon juice
2 cups (225 g) cooked rice, if desired

Place beef shanks, water, tomatoes, celery, onion, garlic, bouillon cubes, salt, pepper and red pepper in Dutch oven. Bring to a boil; reduce heat and simmer, covered, two hours, stirring occasionally. Remove shanks; cut meat from bone into small pieces. Skim fat from broth, if desired. Return meat with cabbage and green pepper to Dutch oven. Continue to simmer, covered, 30 minutes or until meat and vegetables are tender. Stir in lemon juice. To serve, spoon about ¼ cup (60 g) rice into each serving, if desired. Makes eight servings.

Orange Fig-Glazed Duck

Preparation time: 8 minutes
Cooking time: 1 hour 20 minutes

4 to 5 pound (1.8 to 2.25 *kg*) duck
½ teaspoon (2 *g*) salt
¼ teaspoon (1 *g*) pepper
½ teaspoon (2 *g*) rosemary
1 stalk celery, diced
½ medium onion, diced
1 clove garlic, minced
1 tablespoon (15 *g*) parsley, minced
1 orange, peeled, seeded, diced
¼ cup water
  Orange Fig Glaze

Rinse duck and remove excess fat from cavities. Sprinkle inside with salt, pepper and rosemary. Combine celery, onion, garlic, parsley and orange. Loosely stuff duck. Prick duck skin ¼ inch (5 *mm*) deep all over with a sharp-tined fork, especially around thighs and wings, being careful not to pierce meat. Place duck, breast side up, on rack in shallow open roasting-pan. Add water to pan to prevent splattering. Roast at 450°F (230°C) for 20 minutes, then reduce heat to 350°F (180°C) and roast 45 minutes longer.

Meanwhile, prepare *Orange Fig Glaze*. In a small heavy saucepan, combine sugars and cornstarch (cornflour), blending well. Stir in orange juice, grated orange peel and figs. Cook and stir until smooth and thickened, about three minutes. Drain water from roasting pan. Brush duck with glaze and return to oven for 15 minutes until duck is glazed and juices run clear when pricked with a fork. To serve, cut into quarters and pass remaining sauce separately. Makes four servings.

Orange Fig Glaze

⅓ cup (75 *g*) granulated sugar
⅓ cup (75 *g*) brown sugar, packed
1 tablespoon (15 *g*) cornstarch (cornflour)
1½ cups (350 *ml*) orange juice
  Grated peel of one orange
½ cup (75 *g*) snipped dried figs

Potato-Chicken Casserole

Preparation: 5 minutes
Cooking time: 55 to 65 minutes

    1 clove garlic
 ¼ cup (60 g) butter or margarine
    3 tablespoons (40 g) flour
    1 teaspoon (5 g) *each* ground coriander and crushed
       oregano
      Salt and pepper to taste
    3 cups (750 ml) milk or cream
    6 cups (1½ pounds/900 g) russet potatoes, pared and
       thinly sliced
    2 cups (300 g) shredded cooked chicken
    1 can (7 ounces/200 g) chopped green chilies
    1 cup (100 g) shredded Cheddar cheese
 ¼ to ½ cup (30 to 60 g) chopped scallions
       (spring onions)
      Bottled chili salsa

Sauté garlic in butter in saucepan; stir in flour and seasonings. Stir in milk; cook and stir until thickened. Layer half of potatoes in bottom of a two-quart (2 l) baking dish. Distribute chicken and chilies evenly over potato layer; cover with milk mixture. Bake at 350°F (180°C) 40 to 45 minutes or until potatoes are tender. Sprinkle with cheese and scallions; bake at 350°F (180°C) five to ten minutes or until cheese melts. Serve with salsa. Makes six to eight servings.

Tarragon Chicken with Peaches

Preparation time: 3 minutes
Cooking time: 16 to 18 minutes

    1 egg
 ¼ cup (30 g) flour
 ¼ teaspoon (1 g) *each* salt and pepper
    1 whole chicken breast, boned and split
    2 tablespoons (30 ml) vegetable oil
 1½ teaspoons (7 g) tarragon, crumbled
    2 tablespoons (30 ml) brandy*
 ½ cup (120 ml) white wine*
    1 tablespoon (15 g) butter
    1 large or 2 small fresh peaches, sliced

Break egg into shallow container and beat with fork. Combine flour, salt and pepper in another shallow container. Dry chicken and trim off excess fat. Coat chicken with egg, then with flour mixture. Heat oil in a 10-inch (25 cm) frying pan. Sauté chicken, skin side down, over medium-high heat about four minutes or until brown. Turn and brown other side, about three minutes. (Reduce heat to medium if oil starts to burn.)

Sprinkle chicken with tarragon. Add brandy, wine and butter to pan. Bring to boil and cook uncovered two to three minutes to reduce sauce. Add peach slices, cover and cook two to three minutes until fruit is hot. Garnish with parsley, if desired. Makes two servings.

*For a non-alcoholic recipe substitute lemon juice for brandy and water for wine.

Microwave Broccoli and Chicken

Preparation time: 10 minutes
Cooking time: 16 to 18 minutes

2 to 2½ pounds (900 g to 1.13 kg) chicken breasts,
   skinned and boned
   Salt and pepper
2 packages (10 ounces/560 g each) frozen broccoli
   spears (frozen asparagus spears or whole green
   beans may be substituted)
1 tablespoon (15 g) cornstarch (cornflour)

¾ cup (180 ml) orange juice
¾ teaspoon (4 g) marjoram, crushed
½ teaspoon (3 g) grated orange peel or lemon peel
¼ to ½ teaspoon (1 to 2 g) ground ginger
1 can (11 ounces/310 g) mandarin oranges, drained
   Hot cooked rice

Cut chicken breasts diagonally into one-inch (2 cm) slices. Arrange slices in circular pattern in a 9-inch (23 cm) round microwave-safe baking dish; season with salt and pepper. Cut broccoli into two-inch (5 cm) lengths; arrange over chicken. Cover with plastic wrap; microcook on high power 12 to 14 minutes, rotating dish ¼ turn every five minutes. Drain ¼ cup (60 ml) liquid from baking dish into a four-cup (450 ml) microwave-safe container. Cover chicken and broccoli to retain heat; set aside.

Combine cornstarch (cornflour), orange juice, marjoram, orange peel and salt to taste. Add to reserved liquid. Microcook on high for three minutes; stir after two minutes. Add oranges; microcook on high for one minute. Arrange chicken, broccoli and rice on serving platter; spoon sauce over. Makes six servings.

Chicken Chili Bake

Preparation time: 5 minutes
Cooking time: 42 to 45 minutes

2 cans (16 ounces/900 g *each*) cling peach slices in juice or extra light syrup
2 tablespoons (30 g) butter
½ teaspoon (2 g) ground cumin
1 teaspoon (5 g) salt
1½ cups (190 g) yellow cornmeal
2 eggs
1 cup (125 g) chopped onion
1 clove garlic, minced
1 teaspoon (5 g) chili powder
1 teaspoon (5 g) oregano

1½ cups (225 g) shredded cooked chicken
1 package (10 ounces/185 g) frozen corn, thawed
1 can (16 ounces/450 g) stewed tomatoes
1 can (4 ounces/450 g) diced green chilies
½ cup (115 g) chopped green bell pepper
¼ cup (50 g) cilantro leaves
½ teaspoon (2 ml) hot pepper sauce
2 tablespoons (30 g) cornstarch (cornflour)
1 cup (25 g) shredded Monterey Jack (Double Gloucester) cheese (for extra spicy flavor use pepper Monterey Jack cheese)

Drain peaches, reserving all liquid. Add water to reserved liquid to measure 1¼ cups (300 ml), if needed. Bring liquid to a boil. Stir in one tablespoon butter (15 g), cumin, ½ teaspoon salt (2 g) and cornmeal. Remove from heat. Beat in eggs; mix well. Spread evenly over bottom and sides of a 7 × 11-inch (180 × 280 cm), two-quart (2 l) capacity baking dish.

Sauté onion and garlic in a 10-inch (25 cm) frying pan with remaining one tablespoon (15 g) butter. Stir in chili powder, oregano, remaining ½ teaspoon (2 g) salt,

chicken, corn, stewed tomatoes, green chilies, green bell pepper, cilantro and, if desired, hot pepper sauce. Stir together cornstarch (cornflour) and two tablespoons (30 ml) water; stir into chicken mixture. Cook over medium heat until mixture boils and thickens. Stir in peaches and ¾ cup (95 g) cheese. Spoon into prepared dish.

Bake at 350°F (180°C) for 30 minutes or until heated through. Sprinkle with remaining ¼ cup (30 g) cheese during last five minutes of cooking. Makes six servings.

Baked Artichokes Barcelona-Style

Preparation time: 5 minutes
Cooking time: 45 minutes

⅓ cup (80 g) *each* chopped onion and green pepper
2 cloves garlic, minced
2 tablespoons (30 *ml*) olive oil or vegetable oil
6 ounces (170 *g*) *each* boneless chicken chunks and
    bulk Italian sausage
¾ cup (140 *g*) rice

1 can (14 ounces/415 *ml*) chicken broth
½ cup (115 *g*) frozen peas, thawed
1 tomato, peeled and finely chopped
4 cooked artichokes
  Water

To cook fresh artichokes, trim stem flush with petals. Place artichokes in a pot and cover with water. Bring to a vigorous boil and cover. Reduce heat to prevent water from boiling over.

Sauté onion, green pepper and garlic in oil until onion is tender. Add chicken and sausage; cook and stir until browned. Drain excess fat. Stir in rice; cook and stir two minutes. Add broth; simmer covered for 20 minutes. Stir in peas and tomato.

Remove artichokes from heat and plunge in cold water. Remove center petals and chokes from artichokes; discard. Fill artichokes with rice mixture. Place in baking dish; add ½ inch (1 *cm*) water.

Bake uncovered at 350°F (180°C) about 15 minutes or until filling is thoroughly heated. Makes four main dish servings. Recipe can be halved.

Chicken Pesto Roll-Ups

Preparation time: 8 minutes
Cooking time: 7 to 9 minutes

3 chicken breasts, skinned and boned
  Salt and pepper
¾ cup (180 *ml*) *Spinach Pesto Sauce*
2 ounces (60 *g*) Monterey Jack (Double Gloucester)
  cheese, cut into 6 strips
¼ cup (60 *ml*) butter or margarine, melted
¼ cup (25 *g*) seasoned bread crumbs
1 package (16 ounces) or 4 cups (450 *g*) frozen mixed
  vegetables of your choice

Cut each chicken breast in half; place between two pieces of plastic wrap and pound to ¼-inch (½ *cm*). Salt and pepper to taste. Spread chicken breasts with *Spinach Pesto Sauce;* top with strips of cheese. Roll chicken and secure with toothpicks. Dip each roll in butter, coat with bread crumbs and place seam-side down around edge of eight-inch (20 *cm*) microwave-safe baking dish. Microcook, covered with wax paper, at medium-high for seven to nine minutes or until chicken is opaque. Rotate dish after five minutes. Cook mixed vegetables according to package directions; arrange around roll-ups on serving platter. Makes six servings.

Spinach Pesto Sauce

Preparation time: 7 minutes

1 package (10 ounces/275 *g*) or 2 cups (225 *g*) frozen
  chopped spinach
⅔ cup (30 *g*) grated Parmesan cheese
½ cup (120 *ml*) olive oil
⅓ cup (15 *g*) chopped parsley
1 tablespoon (15 *g*) dried basil
1 to 2 cloves garlic
½ teaspoon (2 *g*) salt
1 pinch pepper

Microcook spinach the minimum time given on package directions. Thoroughly drain in sieve by pressing out excess moisture; spread spinach on double layer of paper towels about five minutes. Purée spinach and the rest of the ingredients in a food processor or blender for about 30 seconds. Makes about 1½ cups (375 *g*).

Turkey Corn Chowder

Preparation time: 4 minutes
Cooking time: 45 minutes

1 large onion, chopped
3 tablespoons (45 *ml*) oil
1 pound (45 *kg*) ground turkey meat
1 can (12 ounces/350 *g*) whole kernel corn
1 large potato, peeled and diced
1 can (16 ounces/450 *g*) tomatoes
1½ teaspoons (7 *g*) salt
 ½ teaspoon (2 *g*) pepper
 2 teaspoons (10 *g*) sugar
 3 cups (700 *ml*) boiling water
⅔ cup (160 *ml*) canned evaporated milk

Sauté onion in oil in Dutch oven until transparent. Push to one side. Add turkey meat and cook, stirring, until lightly browned. Add all remaining ingredients *except* canned milk. Stir well. Cover. Bring just to a boil, reduce heat and simmer for 30 minutes or until potatoes are tender. Just before serving remove from heat and slowly stir in evaporated milk. Makes six generous servings.

Roast Turkey Breast Encore

Preparation time: 8 minutes
Cooking time: 45 to 60 minutes

½ turkey breast (about 3 pounds/1.35 *kg*)
⅓ cup (80 *ml*) melted butter
 1 clove fresh garlic, minced
½ teaspoon (2 *g*) thyme

Combine melted butter, garlic and thyme; baste turkey breast. Roast at 450°F (230°C) for 10 minutes; baste with remaining sauce. Reduce heat to 350°F (180°C); continue roasting 35 to 50 minutes or until meat thermometer registers 170°F (76°C). Makes four servings with leftovers. Reserve one to two cups (150 to 300 *g*) for *Creamy Pasta Primavera with Turkey*.

Creamy Pasta Primavera with Turkey

Preparation time: 5 minutes
Cooking time: 10 to 12 minutes

2 tablespoons (30 *ml*) olive oil
1 clove fresh garlic, minced
2 scallions (spring onions), chopped
½ pound (250 *g*) broccoli, cut in florets
2 zucchini (courgette), sliced
¼ pound (125 *g*) snow peas
1 carrot, julienne sliced
1 to 2 cups (150 to 300 *g*) chopped turkey
2 tablespoons (15 *g*) fresh parsley, finely chopped *or*
    ½ teaspoon (5 *g*) dried parsley
2 tablespoons (15 *g*) fresh basil, finely chopped *or*
    ½ teaspoon (5 *g*) dried basil
8 ounces (185 *g*) curly noodles
¼ cup (60 *ml*) heavy cream
   Salt and pepper to taste
¼ cup (30 *g*) grated Parmesan cheese

In hot oil, sauté garlic, onions, broccoli and zucchini for three minutes. Add ¼ cup (60 *ml*) water; cover and steam four minutes. Stir in snow peas, carrot, turkey, parsley and basil. Cook, stirring until hot and toss with hot, drained noodles. Combine with cream and seasonings; sprinkle with cheese. Makes four servings.

44

Turkey Fondue with Three Dipping Sauces

Preparation time: 5 minutes
Cooking time: 5 to 7 minutes

1 pound (450 g) turkey breast steaks, about ½ inch
   (2 cm) thickness
2 tablespoons (30 g) butter
1 tablespoon (15 ml) oil
¾ teaspoon (3 g) seasoned salt
1 pinch pepper
2 tablespoons (30 ml) dry sherry
1 tablespoon (15 g) chopped parsley
  Dipping sauces, prepared in advance

Cut turkey into one-inch (3 cm) squares. Heat butter and oil in large frying pan. Add turkey, and brown quickly, turning once. Turkey should cook only about two minutes altogether. Sprinkle with salt and pepper, add sherry, and bring to a boil. Sprinkle with parsley, and serve at once with the following dipping sauces: *Sour Cream Dip, Sesame Curry Mayonnaise, Spicy Catsup*. Makes four servings.

Sour Cream Dip

1 cup (225 g) dairy sour cream
¼ cup (15 g) crumbled bleu (Stilton) cheese
½ teaspoon (2 g) salt
¼ teaspoon (1 g) onion powder
1 tablespoon (15 g) chopped parsley
1 pinch white pepper
2 drops Tabasco sauce

Blend together all the ingredients. Chill an hour or so to blend flavors. Makes about 1 cup (250 g).

Sesame Curry Mayonnaise

1 cup (225 g) mayonnaise
1 tablespoon (15 g) *each* finely chopped onion and
  green pepper
½ teaspoon (2 g) curry powder
1 tablespoon (15 g) toasted sesame seeds

Blend together all the ingredients. Chill an hour or so to blend flavors. Makes about 1 cup (250 g).

Spicy Catsup

1 cup catsup (225 g)
2 teaspoons (10 g) *each* prepared mustard and tarragon
  wine vinegar
1 pinch dill weed

Blend together all the ingredients. Chill an hour or so to blend flavors. Makes about 1 cup (250 g).

Hot and Sour Turkey Wings

Preparation time: 5 minutes
Cooking time: 35 to 37 minutes

4 turkey wings (4 pounds/1.8 *kg*)
2 tablespoons (30 *ml*) oil
1 can (20 ounces/570 *g*) pineapple chunks
¼ cup (60 *ml*) soy sauce
2 tablespoons (30 *ml*) vinegar
1 tablespoon (15 *g*) sugar
1 clove fresh garlic, minced
2 teaspoons (10 *g*) dried red pepper flakes
½ teaspoon (2 *g*) ground ginger
1 cup (100 *g*) scallion (spring onion) fans
1 red or green bell pepper, cut into strips
1 tablespoon (15 *g*) toasted sesame seeds

Cut each wing into two pieces, leaving tip with blade. Brown slowly on all sides in large wok or Dutch oven in heated oil. Drain excess fat. Combine ⅓ cup (80 *ml*) syrup or juice from pineapple with soy sauce, vinegar, sugar, garlic, red pepper flakes and ginger. Pour over turkey wings; simmer, covered, 20 minutes or until tender. Add pineapple chunks, scallion fans and pepper strips. Simmer 10 minutes. Sprinkle sesame seeds over dish. Makes four to six servings.

Note: To make scallion fans, cut 1½-inch (4 *cm*) lengths of scallions, then cut both ends in several lengthwise cuts. Place in ice water to curl ends.

Honey Barbecue Sauce

Preparation time: 2 minutes
Cooking time: 10 minutes

1 can (15 ounces/400 *g*) condensed tomato soup
½ cup (125 *g*) honey
2 tablespoons (30 *ml*) Worcestershire sauce
2 to 3 tablespoons (30 to 45 *ml*) vegetable oil
1 tablespoon (15 *ml*) lemon juice
1 teaspoon (5 *g*) prepared mustard
1 pinch cayenne *or* dash bottled hot pepper sauce
   optional

In a saucepan, combine all ingredients and bring to a boil. Reduce heat and simmer, uncovered, five minutes. Makes about two cups (450 *g*).

Barbecued Salmon and Mushroom Packets

Preparation time: 6 minutes
Cooking time: 10 to 15 minutes

4 (about 6 ounces/170 g) *each* salmon steaks or
    fillets, thawed if necessary
3 tablespoons (45 *ml*) butter or margarine, melted
1 pinch *each* salt, pepper and rosemary, crushed
2 tablespoons (30 *ml*) dry vermouth or dry white
    wine
1 cup (125 g) sliced mushrooms
2 tablespoons (30 g) minced scallions (spring onions)
    Barbecued Corn on the Cob

Cut four 12-inch (30 *cm*) squares of heavy duty or
double thickness aluminum foil; grease top surface.
Place salmon steaks on foil. Combine butter, seasonings
and vermouth; stir in mushrooms and scallions. Divide
mushroom mixture over salmon; seal foil tightly. If your
barbecue is further than your backyard, transport
packets to picnic site in an ice chest.
Barbecue on grill or directly on medium hot coals.
Cook 10 to 15 minutes or until salmon flakes easily when
tested with a fork; turn packets every five minutes. Serve
with *Barbecued Corn on the Cob*. Makes four servings.

Barbecued Corn on the Cob

Preparation time: 10 to 12 minutes
Cooking time: 15 to 20 minutes

6 ears sweet corn or frozen corn on the cob, thawed
    butter or margarine
    Salt and pepper to taste

Peel back the husks from six ears of sweet corn;
remove corn silk. Brush with softened butter or margarine; season with salt and pepper. Replace husk around
corn. Place on heavy duty or double thickness aluminum
foil; sprinkle each ear with ½ teaspoon (5 g) water. Wrap
tightly. Place on grill or directly on medium hot coals and
barbecue about 15 to 20 minutes or until tender; turn
frequently. Makes four servings.

Poached Salmon and Winter Vegetables with Lemon Sauce

Preparation time: 7 minutes
Cooking time: 10 to 15 minutes

4 cups (900 *ml*) water
1 small onion cut in slices lengthwise
10 peppercorns
½ lemon, sliced
1 bay leaf
2 cups *each* (250 g *each*) broccoli florets and
    cauliflorets, cooked until crisp-tender
2 salmon steaks (6 to 8 ounces *each*/100 to 150 g
    each), thawed if necessary
Lemon Sauce

Bring water to boil in frying pan with cover. Reduce heat and add peppercorns, lemon slices and bay leaf; simmer five minutes. Add salmon steaks to liquid. Cover and simmer 10 minutes per inch (2 *cm*) of thickness or until fish flakes when tested with a fork. Arrange fish and hot cooked vegetables on platter; drizzle salmon with *Lemon Sauce*. Serve with remaining *Lemon Sauce*. Makes two servings.

Note: For a delicious, low-calorie alternative to high cholesterol sauces for fish, try the *Creamy Lemon Garlic Sauce.*

Lemon Sauce

Preparation time: 6 minutes
Cooking time: 2 minutes

2 eggs
2 tablespoons (30 *ml*) light cream
¼ teaspoon (1 g) salt
2 tablespoons (30 *ml*) lemon juice
1 tablespoon (15 g) butter or margarine

Beat eggs until light and frothy; add light cream and salt. Gradually add lemon juice; beat constantly. Cook and stir over low heat until thickened. Stir in butter. Makes about ½ cup (125 g).

Creamy Lemon Garlic Sauce
(not pictured)

¼ cup (60 g) plain nonfat yogurt
¼ cup (60 g) light mayonnaise
1 teaspoon (5 g) lemon juice
1 clove garlic, pressed in garlic press

In a mixing bowl, whisk together all the ingredients well. Chill until ready to serve. Makes (½ cup/125 g) four to six servings.

Poached Whole Salmon with Three Sauces

Preparation time: 8 to 10 minutes
Cooking time: 35 to 60 minutes

1 whole salmon (4 to 6 pounds/1.8 to 2.75 *kg*), thawed if necessary
1 lemon, halved
2 slices onion
1 teaspoon (5 *g*) salt
8 peppercorns
  Boiling water
  Garnish: Lemon and cucumber slices and dill weed
  Remoulade Sauce, *Cucumber Sauce* and *Dill Sauce*

Rinse salmon; remove head and tail if desired. Wrap the fish in cheesecloth leaving long ends on the cloth to serve as handles for removing the fish from poaching liquid. Place salmon in large roasting or poaching pan. Squeeze juice from lemon half; pour over fish. Slice remaining lemon half; place over fish with onion, salt and peppercorns. Add enough boiling water to cover salmon, and cover pan with lid or aluminum foil.

Bake at 425°F (220°C) or simmer on top of range allowing 10 to 12 minutes per inch (2 *cm*) of thickness measured at its thickest part or eight to ten minutes per pound (500 *g*) or until salmon flakes easily when tested with a fork. Remove salmon from liquid; gently remove skin while warm. Garnish with lemon and cucumber slices and dill weed. Serve with *Remoulade Sauce*, *Cucumber Sauce* and *Dill Sauce*. Makes 12 to 18 servings.

Remoulade Sauce

1 cup (225 *g*) mayonnaise
1 tablespoon (15 *g*) minced parsley
1 tablespoon (15 *g*) chopped dill pickle
2 teaspoons (30 *g*) minced shallots or scallions (spring onions)
1 teaspoon (15 *g*) chopped capers
2 minced anchovy fillets
¼ teaspoon (1 *g*) crushed chervil or tarragon

Cucumber Sauce

1 cup (125 *g*) chopped cucumber
¼ cup (30 *g*) chopped mild onion
2 tablespoons (30 *ml*) *each* white vinegar and vegetable oil
¼ teaspoon (1 *g*) *each* salt and coarsely ground black pepper

Dill Sauce

1 cup (225 *g*) dairy sour cream or half-and-half
½ teaspoon (2 *g*) crushed dill weed
  Salt and pepper to taste

Combine the ingredients in a small mixing bowl. Chill at least one hour to blend flavors. Makes about 1¼ cups (225 *g*).

Salmon Chowder Au Gratin

Preparation time: 5 minutes
Cooking time: 35 minutes

1 can (15½ ounces/250 g) salmon
½ cup (60 g) chopped celery
2 tablespoons (30 g) butter or margarine
2 tablespoons (30 g) flour
2¼ cups (310 ml) milk
2 cups (250 g) cauliflower florets, cooked until tender
1 package (10 ounces/275 g) frozen peas
½ teaspoon (2 g) dill weed, crushed
¼ teaspoon (1 g) salt
1 cup (125 g) shredded Cheddar cheese
1 cup (125 g) shredded Swiss cheese

Drain salmon, reserving liquid; flake with a fork. Sauté onions and celery in butter or margarine until tender; blend in flour. Gradually stir in reserved salmon liquid and milk; heat to boiling. Stir in cauliflower florets, peas, salmon, dill weed and salt. Heat through until hot; stir in cheeses, stirring constantly until melted. Makes about six servings.

Salmon Steaks

Preparation time: 5 minutes
Cooking time: 25 minutes

1 tablespoon (15 ml) olive oil
1 tablespoon (15 g) butter or margarine
1 or 2 teaspoons (5 to 8 g) minced garlic
¼ cup (30 g) chopped scallions (spring onions)
2 tablespoons (30 ml) lemon juice
1 tablespoon (15 g) minced fresh dill
4 (6 to 8 ounces each/170 to 225 g each) salmon steaks,
    thawed if necessary
Minced parsley

Heat butter and oil until butter melts; sauté garlic. Add scallions, lemon juice and dill. Spoon over salmon. Bake at 350°F (180°C) for 15 minutes or until fish flakes when tested with a fork. Garnish with parsley. Makes four servings.

Salmon Corn Chowder

Preparation time: 2 minutes
Cooking time: 8 to 10 minutes

1 can (15½ ounces/435 g) salmon
⅔ cup (80 g) chopped celery
½ cup (60 g) frozen chopped onions
2 tablespoons (30 g) butter or margarine
2 cans (10¾ ounces each/300 g each) condensed
    cream of celery soup

2½ cups (570 ml) milk
1 can (16½ ounces/450 g) cream-style corn
¾ cup (100 g) frozen cut corn
    Paprika

Drain salmon, reserving liquid; flake. Sauté celery and onion in butter until tender. Add condensed soup, milk and salmon liquid. Heat and stir until smooth. Add salmon, cream-style corn and cut corn. Cook until heated through. Sprinkle with paprika before serving. Makes six servings.

Halibut Stew

Preparation time: 8 minutes
Cooking time: 35 minutes

2 pounds (1 *kg*) halibut, thawed if necessary
6 hard-shelled clams or 1 can (6½ ounces/125 *g*)
   chopped clams
1 cup (125 *g*) chopped onion
¾ cup (90 *g*) *each* chopped celery and carrot
½ cup (60 *g*) chopped green pepper
1 clove garlic, minced
2 tablespoons (30 *ml*) olive oil

1 can (29 ounces/800 *g*) tomatoes
1 cup (250 *ml*) *each* tomato juice and white wine or
   water
¼ teaspoon (2 *g*) *each* sweet basil and oregano leaves,
   crushed
  Salt and pepper
1 tablespoon (15 *g*) chopped parsley

Cut halibut into 1-inch (3 *cm*) pieces. Sauté onion, celery, carrot, green pepper and garlic in olive oil. Add tomatoes, tomato juice, wine or water and herbs. Simmer, covered, 20 minutes. Add halibut and clams. Simmer, covered, 5 to 10 minutes longer or until halibut flakes easily when tested with a fork and clams are opened. Discard any clams that do not open. Salt and pepper to taste. Sprinkle with chopped parsley. Makes six to eight servings.

Creole Halibut over Rice

Preparation time: 6 minutes
Cooking time: 40 to 45 minutes

2 pounds (1 *kg*) halibut, thawed if necessary and
  boned and skinned
½ cup (60 g) *each* chopped onion, green pepper and
  celery
1 clove garlic
2 tablespoons (30 *g*) butter or margarine
1 can (15 ounces/425 *g*) tomato sauce

½ cup (120 *ml*) water
½ teaspoon (2 *g*) thyme, crushed
1 bay leaf
1 teaspoon (5 *g*) salt
1 pinch pepper
  Steamed rice
1 tablespoon (15 *g*) chopped parsley

Cut halibut into bite-sized pieces. Sauté onion, green pepper, celery and garlic in butter. Add tomato sauce, water and seasonings. Simmer, covered, 20 minutes. Meanwhile, place halibut on an oiled broiling pan. Broil, allowing about 10 minutes per inch (2 *cm*) of thickness of fish measured at its thickest part or until halibut flakes when tested with a fork. Remove bay leaf from tomato sauce. Add halibut to sauce and heat thoroughly. Serve over steamed rice; garnish with chopped parsley. Makes four to six servings.

Tuscan White Fish

Preparation time: 7 minutes
Cooking time: 25 to 30 minutes

1½ cups (185 g) pitted black olives, drained
1 medium tomato, seeded and finely chopped
½ cup (60 g) finely chopped celery
1½ teaspoons (5 g) oregano, crumbled
2 pinches pepper
1 to 2 bunches fresh parsley
4 servings (about 1¼ pounds/600 g) sole, cod or
  other white fish

½ cup (25 g) grated Parmesan cheese
⅓ cup (75 g) dairy sour cream
1 medium clove garlic
1 tablespoon (15 g) dried basil
½ cup (120 ml) vegetable oil
  Garnish: Tomato wedges and lemon slices

Reserve ⅓ cup (75 g) olives. Chop remaining olives and combine with tomato, celery, oregano, pepper and ½ cup (115 g) minced parsley. Spoon equal amounts onto fish fillets. Roll fish around filling. Place seam-side down in shallow 1½-quart (1.5-l) baking dish. Cover and bake in a 400°F (200°C) oven for 25 minutes or until fish is done.

Meanwhile, make sauce: Combine 1 cup (packed) (50 g) parsley sprigs with cheese, sour cream, garlic and basil in electric blender. Whir on and off until smooth and blended. Turn into saucepan. Heat gently until warm but *don't boil*. Spoon over fish to serve. Garnish with reserved whole olives, the tomato wedges and lemon slices as desired. Makes four servings.

Glazed Leg of Lamb

Preparation time: 10 minutes
Cooking time: 1 hour 30 minutes

½ leg of lamb, sirloin (rump) end,
  (about 4½ pounds/2 *kg*)
  Salt
  Thyme
  Lemon pepper
½ cup (150 *g*) corn syrup or honey
¼ cup (60 *ml*) red wine vinegar
2 tablespoons (30 *g*) catsup

Place lamb, fat side up, in shallow roasting pan. Sprinkle with salt, thyme and lemon pepper. Rub seasonings into lamb surface. In a small bowl, stir together corn syrup, red wine vinegar and catsup until smooth. Use to baste lamb last 30 minutes of roasting. Roast lamb in preheated 325°F (160°C) for rare, 150°F to 155°F (65°C to 68°C) for medium or 160°F (70°C) for medium-well. Makes four servings.

Lamb and Macaroni Casserole

Preparation time: 30 to 45 minutes
Cooking time: 1 hour 30 minutes

 1 pound (450 *g*) ground lamb
1½ cups (340 *g*) elbow macaroni
 5 tablespoons (70 *g*) butter or margarine, divided
⅓ cup (40 *g*) flour
 3 cups (700 *ml*) milk
½ cup (25 *g*) grated kefalotiri or Parmesan cheese
½ cup (25 *g*) finely chopped onion
 2 cloves garlic, minced
 1 tablespoon (15 *ml*) olive oil
½ teaspoon (2 *g*) dried oregano leaves
¼ teaspoon (1 *g*) salt
¼ teaspoon (1 *g*) ground cinnamon
 1 pinch freshly ground pepper
 1 pinch nutmeg
 1 can (10 ounces/280 *g*) tomatoes
¼ cup (75 *g*) tomato paste
 4 eggs
⅓ cup (15 *g*) soft bread crumbs

Prepare macaroni according to package directions; drain. Rinse with cold water and drain; set aside. Stir flour into 4 tablespoons melted butter (60 *g*) in heavy saucepan. Gradually stir in milk and cook until thickened, stirring occasionally. Add cheese and stir until melted. Cover and cool slightly.

Brown ground lamb, onion and garlic in olive oil in large frying pan. Pour off drippings. Sprinkle oregano, salt, cinnamon, pepper and nutmeg over lamb. Break up tomatoes and drain liquid into small bowl; reserve tomatoes. Combine tomato liquid and tomato paste; stir into lamb mixture and cook over medium heat five minutes. Stir in tomatoes.

Separate one egg; combine yolk and 1 cup (250 *ml*) white sauce in small bowl; reserve. Beat together egg white, remaining three eggs and remaining white sauce in large bowl; gently stir in macaroni. A wooden spoon works best for this. Place half of the macaroni mixture in bottom of a buttered 8 × 8-inch (20 × 20 *cm*) baking dish. Spoon lamb mixture in an even layer over macaroni; place remaining macaroni mixture over lamb. Pour reserved white sauce and egg yolk mixture over macaroni. Stir bread crumbs into 1 tablespoon (15 *g*) melted butter; sprinkle over top.

Bake in a moderate oven (375°F or 190°C) 45 minutes. Reduce oven temperature to 325°F (160°C) and continue baking 15 minutes. Let stand 15 minutes before serving. Makes six servings.

Lamb Steaks with Scalloped Apples and Carrots

Preparation time: 8 to 10 minutes
Cooking time: 55 minutes

3 or 4 lamb steaks, cut 1-inch (2 *cm*) thick
2 tablespoons (30 *g*) butter
¼ cup (40 *g*) chopped onions
1 cup (180 *ml*) apple juice or chicken stock
3 tablespoons (45 *g*) brown sugar
1 tablespoon (15 *g*) chopped candied ginger (optional)
1 teaspoon (5 *g*) salt
¼ teaspoon (1 *g*) ground allspice (mixed spice)
1 pinch ground nutmeg
1 pinch ground cinnamon
2 Granny Smith apples, peeled, sliced
2 carrots, peeled, sliced on diagonal
1 tablespoon (15 *mg*) cornstarch (cornflour)

In a large frying pan, brown steaks on both sides in hot butter. Add onions and sauté until soft. Drain excess oil. Add ¾ cup (135 *ml*) of the apple juice, brown sugar, ginger, salt and spices. Cover and simmer 25 minutes.

Add apple and carrot slices. Cover and simmer 15 minutes. Remove steaks to warm platter.

Stir cornstarch (cornflour) into remaining ¼ cup (45 *ml*) apple juice; stir into frying pan juices. Bring to boil and stir until thickened and smooth. Pour scalloped apples and carrots over lamb steaks.

Note: The carrots cooked in this manner will be al dente, slightly crisp. For very soft carrots, cook in salted boiling water 5 minutes before adding to lamb.

Apricot-Glazed Lamb Steaks

Preparation time: 10 minutes
Cooking time: 14 to 16 minutes

4 lamb shoulder arm or blade chops, cut ¾-inch (2 *cm*) thick
⅓ cup (80 *ml*) apricot jam
1 tablespoon (15 *ml*) white vinegar
1 teaspoon (5 *g*) Dijon-style mustard
½ teaspoon (2 *g*) *each* crushed rosemary and salt
1 clove garlic, minced
¼ teaspoon (1 *g*) pepper

Combine apricot jam, vinegar, mustard, rosemary, salt, garlic and pepper in a small saucepan and cook slowly, stirring until melted. Place lamb shoulder chops on grill over medium coals.* Broil 14 to 16 minutes for medium, turning once. Brush both sides with glaze several times during cooking. Makes four to five servings.

*Test about four inches (10 *cm*) above coals for medium with a four-second hand count.

Sorrel and Lamb Soup

Preparation time: 8 minutes
Cooking time: 1 hour 20 minutes to 1½ hours

1½ to 2 pounds (650 to 900 *g*) lamb riblets
  2 tablespoons (30 *ml*) oil
  2 medium potatoes, peeled, diced
  3 medium carrots, thickly sliced
  2 leeks, washed, sliced
  2 quarts (8 cups/1.75 *l*) chicken stock
  1 teaspoon (5 *g*) dill weed
  1 teaspoon (5 *g*) tarragon
  1 teaspoon (5 *g*) celery salt
½ teaspoon (2 *g*) ground black pepper
  1 to 2 tablespoons (30 *ml*) lemon juice
  4 cups (8 ounces/250 *g*) chopped sorrel

Brown lamb on all sides in hot oil. Drain.
Add potatoes, carrots, leeks, chicken stock and seasonings. Simmer, covered, for one hour. Stir in lemon juice and sorrel. Simmer 15 to 20 minutes. Correct seasoning, as desired. Makes six to eight servings.

Note: Meat may be removed from bones before serving. Soup freezes well.

Seasoned Lamb Chops

Preparation time: 20 minutes
Cooking time: 1 hour 15 minutes

4 lamb shoulder blade or arm chops (or chump chops),
    cut ¾ inch (2 *cm*) thick
2 tablespoons (30 *ml*) olive oil
1 teaspoon (5 *g*) salt
1 pinch freshly ground black pepper
½ cup (120 *ml*) white wine
1 bay leaf
1 large clove garlic, minced
⅛ teaspoon ground allspice (pinch mixed spice)
2 medium onions, quartered
1 package (10 ounces/160 *g*) frozen asparagus spears,
    separated
1 cup (125 *g*) quartered mushrooms
2 large tomatoes, peeled, seeded, chopped

Brown lamb chops and garlic in oil in large frying pan;
pour off drippings. Season chops with salt and pepper. Add
wine, bay leaf, garlic and allspice to lamb chops. Cover
tightly and cook slowly 25 to 30 minutes. Add onions and
continue cooking, covered, 15 minutes. Add asparagus and
continue cooking, covered, five to seven minutes. Add
mushrooms and continue cooking, covered, 10 minutes.
Stir in tomatoes and heat through. Remove lamb to warm
platter. Remove vegetables with slotted spoon and arrange
around lamb chops. Makes four servings.

Lamb Chops with Summer Vegetables

Preparation time: 15 minutes
Cooking time: 7 to 11 minutes

4 lamb rib or loin chops, cut 1 inch (3 *cm*) thick
1 clove garlic, cut in half
¼ teaspoon (1 *g*) salt
¼ teaspoon (1 *g*) freshly ground black pepper, divided
12 carrots
1 small yellow squash, diagonally sliced
1 small zucchini (courgette) squash, diagonally sliced
1 tablespoon (15 *g*) butter
1 teaspoon (5 *g*) fresh lemon juice
¼ teaspoon (1 *g*) dill weed

Rub cut sides of garlic over both sides of lamb chops.
Place lamb chops on rack in broiler pan so surface of meat
is three to four inches (7 to 10 *cm*) from heat. Broil three to
five minutes. Season with salt and a pinch of pepper, turn
and continue broiling four to six minutes or to desired
degree of doneness (rare or medium).
Meanwhile, steam carrots seven to eight minutes; add
yellow and zucchini squash and continue steaming one
minute or until tender-crisp. Melt butter; add lemon juice,
remaining pepper and dill weed and drizzle over vegetables.
Serve vegetables with lamb chops. Makes two servings.

Sausage and Vegetable Soup

Preparation time: 15 minutes
Microwave cooking time: 20 minutes

12 ounces 'fully-cooked' smoked pork link sausage, cut
    into ½-inch (12 *mm*) slices
1 medium potato, grated
1 large carrot, cut into thin strips 1½ inches (4 *cm*)
    long
1 medium onion, chopped
3½ cups (825 *ml*) water
¾ teaspoon (3 *g*) salt
¼ teaspoon (1 *g*) celery seed
2 pinches crushed red pepper pods
2 cups (8 to 12 leaves) coarsely chopped cabbage
2 tablespoons (30 *g*) snipped parsley

Combine potato, carrot, onion, water, salt, celery seed
and red pepper in a two-quart (2 *l*) microwave-safe bowl.
Cover with plastic wrap, venting one corner and microwave at high power 12 minutes, stirring every six minutes. Stir cabbage and sausage into vegetables, cover
with plastic wrap, vent and microwave at high four minutes. Stir in parsley, cover with plastic wrap, vent and
microwave at high four minutes. Makes four servings.

Conventional method: Combine smoked sausage, potato,
carrot, onion, water, salt, celery seed and red pepper in a
two-quart (2 *l*) saucepan. Bring to a boil; reduce heat,
cover tightly and simmer 10 minutes. Add cabbage and
cover tightly, simmer five minutes. Stir in parsley and
cover tightly, simmer one minute. Makes four servings.

Grilled Sausage with Sweet Potato and Apple Kabobs

Preparation time: 15 minutes
Cooking time: 15 minutes

1 pound (450 *g*) fresh country-style pork sausage
    links, bratwurst or Polish sausage
¼ cup (75 *g*) apple jelly, melted
½ teaspoon (2 *g*) orange or lemon juice
1 pinch *each* ground allspice (mixed spice) and
    nutmeg
1 large sweet potato (or yam), cut crosswise into
    ¾-inch (2 *cm*) slices (about 12 ounces/300 *g*)
1 large apple, cored, cut into eight wedges
1 tablespoon (15 *g*) butter, melted

Combine jelly, orange juice, allspice and nutmeg. Par-
boil sweet potato in boiling water seven minutes; drain.
Thread sweet potato slices and apple wedges on four 12-
inch (30 *cm*) skewers. Brush lightly with butter. Place
sausages on grill over low to medium coals.* Broil 5
minutes. Place kabobs on grill and brush sausage and
kabobs with apple jelly mixture after five minutes. Inter-
nal temperature of sausage should register 170°F (77°C).
Makes four servings.

*Test about four inches (10 *cm*) above coals for medium
with a five-second hand count.

Quick Sausage Gumbo-Style Soup

Preparation time: 5 minutes
Cooking time: 15 minutes

12 ounces (175 g) 'fully-cooked' Polish sausage, cut into
⅟₂-inch (12 mm) pieces
1 can (16 ounces/450 g) stewed tomatoes
1½ cups (370 ml) water
1 package (10 ounces/325 g) frozen cut okra
1 teaspoon (5 g) dried thyme leaves
¼ teaspoon (1 g) garlic powder
2 teaspoons (10 ml) hot pepper sauce
1 cup (250 g) hot cooked rice

Combine Polish sausage, tomatoes, water, okra, thyme
and garlic powder in a large saucepan. Bring to boil; reduce
heat, cover tightly and simmer eight to ten minutes, stirring
occasionally. (Do not overcook.) Stir in hot pepper sauce.
Ladle each serving over ¼ cup (60 g) rice. Makes four
servings.

Smoked Sausage Dinner

Preparation time: 5 minutes
Cooking time: 18 minutes

12 ounces (350 g) 'fully-cooked' smoked pork link
sausage, cut diagonally into 1-inch (3-cm) pieces
2 tablespoons (30 ml) water
1 medium onion
2 small red cooking apples
2 tablespoons (30 g) butter, divided
12 ounces (350 g) frozen potato wedges
¼ cup (60 ml) cider vinegar
3 tablespoons (45 g) sugar
½ teaspoon (2 g) caraway seed
2 tablespoons (30 g) chopped parsley

Place sausage and water in large non-stick frying pan;
cover tightly and cook over medium heat eight minutes,
stirring occasionally. Meanwhile, cut onion into 12 wedges;
core and cut each apple into eight wedges. Remove sausage
to warm platter. Pour off drippings. Cook and stir onion and
apples in 1 tablespoon (15 g) butter in same frying pan four
minutes or until apples are just tender. Remove to sausage
platter.
Heat remaining butter; add potatoes and cook, covered,
over medium-high heat five minutes or until potatoes are
tender and golden brown, stirring occasionally. Combine
vinegar, sugar and caraway seed. Reduce heat, return sausage, apple mixture and vinegar mixture to frying pan and
cook one minute, or until heated through, stirring gently.
Sprinkle with parsley. Makes four servings.

Spicy Roast Pork and Beans

Preparation time: 7 minutes
Cooking time: 5 hours 30 minutes to 6 hours

1 pound (375 *g*) pinto, small red, kidney or pink beans
1 pork roast (3 pounds/1.35 *kg*)
7 cups (1.75 *l*) water
½ cup (80 *g*) chopped onion
2 cloves garlic, minced
1 tablespoon (15 *g*) salt
2 tablespoons (30 *g*) chili powder
1 tablespoon (15 *g*) cumin
1 teaspoon (5 *g*) oregano
1 can (4 ounces/125 *g*) chopped green chilies
1 jar or can (2 ounces/60 *g*) diced pimento
    Corn chips
    Condiments*

Place beans, pork roast, water, onion, garlic seasonings, chilies and pimento in heavy kettle or Dutch oven. Cover and simmer about 5 hours or until roast is fork tender. Remove roast and break up with fork. Return to bean pot. Cook uncovered until thick, about one-half hour. Serve over corn chips. Pass condiments for choice of toppings. Makes 10 to 12 servings.

*Condiments: Diced tomato, diced avocado, sliced scallions (spring onions), grated Cheddar cheese, hot pepper sauce or bottled salsa.

Cranberry-Glazed Ham

Preparation time: 5 minutes
Cooking time: 1 to 1 ½ hours

3 to 4 pound (1.35 to 1.8 *kg*) boneless 'fully-cooked' smoked ham half
1 cup (300 *g*) *each* prepared mincemeat and whole berry cranberry sauce
2 tablespoons (30 *g*) chopped walnuts
1 teaspoon (15 *g*) spicy brown mustard

Do not preheat oven. Place smoked ham half (straight from refrigerator) on rack in shallow roasting pan. Add ½ cup (120 *ml*) water. Insert a meat thermometer into thickest part of ham. Cover pan tightly with aluminum foil, leaving thermometer dial exposed. Roast in 325°F (160°C) slow oven until thermometer registers 135°F (55°C), about 19 to 23 minutes per pound/450 *g*. Meanwhile, combine mincemeat, cranberry sauce, walnuts and mustard. Remove aluminum foil and spread a small amount of the glaze over ham 15 minutes before end of cooking time. Remove ham when the meat thermometer registers 135°F (55°C). Allow ham to stand, covered, about 10 minutes or until thermometer registers 140°F (60°C).

Note: A boneless 'fully-cooked' smoked ham will yield four to five, three-ounce (85 *g*) cooked servings per pound (450 *g*).

Microwave Pasta Primavera
with Smoked Ham

Preparation time: 5 minutes
Cooking time: 10 to 12 minutes

⅓ cup (35 g) blanched slivered almonds
4 ounces (125 g) dry spinach fettucine
1½ cups (375 ml) lowfat milk
1 tablespoon (15 g) cornstarch (cornflour)
1 teaspoon (5 g) Dijon-style mustard
1 cup (125 g) grated Jarlsberg cheese
2 tablespoons (30 g) thinly sliced scallions
    (spring onions)

¼ teaspoon (1 g) black pepper
1 cup (150 g) smoked ham strips
½ cup (175 g) red pepper strips
1 cup (225 g) broccoli florets
1 cup (225 g) cauliflower florets

Spread almonds in single layer on a microwave-safe plate. Microwave on high power for three minutes, stirring halfway through, until almonds are lightly browned. Cool on counter. Cook pasta in boiling water according to package directions. Drain and keep warm.

Meanwhile, whisk together milk, cornstarch (cornflour) and mustard in a large, microwave-safe bowl, until cornstarch (cornflour) is thoroughly dissolved. Cover bowl with waxed paper; microwave on high power for five to six minutes until mixture just boils. Watch carefully, as milk will boil over easily. Remove from oven and whisk until smooth. Whisk in cheese, scallions and pepper, until cheese is melted and sauce is smooth. Stir in ham strips and red pepper strips. Set aside.

Place broccoli and cauliflower florets in microwave-safe plastic bag. Microwave on high power for two minutes, until tender-crisp. Reheat sauce if necessary. Stir in toasted almonds, broccoli and cauliflower florets. Divide pasta between serving bowls. Spoon sauce over pasta to serve. Makes two servings.

Cheesy Pasta Bake

Preparation time: 8 minutes
Cooking time: 1 hour 10 minutes

⅔ cup (70 *g*) chopped almonds
2 cups (300 *g*) chopped onion
2 large cloves garlic, minced
2 tablespoons (30 *g*) butter
2 teaspoons (5 *g*) basil
1 teaspoon (5 *g*) oregano
1 can (16 ounces/450 *g*) stewed tomatoes

1 cup (150 *g*) cooked rice-shaped pasta (orzo)
¾ cup (190 *ml*) milk
2 eggs, beaten
2 cups (250 *g*) shredded Monterey Jack (Double Gloucester) cheese
⅓ cup (40 *g*) grated Romano or Parmesan cheese

Spread almonds in a shallow pan. Toast at 375°F (190°C), 10 minutes or until lightly browned; cool. Sauté onion and garlic in butter. Stir in basil, oregano, stewed tomatoes, pasta, milk, eggs, 1½ cups (185 *g*) Monterey Jack cheese, Romano cheese and ⅓ cup (35 *g*) almonds.

Bake at 375°F (190°C) for one hour. Top with remaining ½ cup (60 *g*) Monterey Jack cheese and ⅓ cup (35 *g*) almonds. Return to oven for five minutes until cheese is melted and bubbly. Makes six to eight servings.

Easy Curried Corn Chowder

Preparation time: 5 minutes
Cooking time: 35 to 40 minutes

1 can (16 ounces/450 *g*) cling peach slices in juice or
   extra light syrup
½ pound (225 *g*) bacon, cut into 1-inch (3 *cm*) pieces
1 onion, thinly sliced
¼ cup (30 *g*) flour
2 teaspoons (10 *g*) curry powder
½ cup (60 *g*) *each* chopped celery, red and green
   bell peppers

1 box (10½ ounces/275 *g*) frozen corn kernels,
   thawed
1 large potato, cut into 1-inch (3 *cm*) cubes
2 cans (14½ ounces *each*/815 *ml each*) chicken broth
1 bay leaf
1 cup (250 *ml*) light cream

Drain peaches, reserving all liquid for other uses. Cut slices in half and set aside. Brown bacon in a large saucepan over medium heat. Remove bacon from pan and drain on paper towels. Reserve.

Drain off all but two tablespoons (30 *ml*) fat from pan. Stir in onions; cook until golden brown, about eight minutes. Stir in flour, curry powder, chopped celery and

chopped bell peppers; cook one minute. Stir in corn, potatoes, chicken broth and bay leaf. Bring to a boil, whisking occasionally. Simmer 20 minutes, until potatoes are tender. Remove from heat. Remove bay leaf; stir in cream and reserved peaches. Ladle soup into serving bowls. Top with reserved crisp bacon just before serving. Makes six servings.

Potato-Tomato Bake

Preparation time: 6 minutes
Cooking time: 30 minutes

2½ pounds (about 5 medium) russet potatoes (1125 g), pared and sliced ¼-inch (5 mm) thick
⅓ cup (50 g) thinly sliced onion
½ teaspoon (2 g) salt
¼ teaspoon (1 g) basil, crushed

1 pinch pepper
1 cup shredded Swiss cheese
1 tomato (125 g), peeled and thinly sliced
⅔ cup (160 ml) tomato juice
2 tablespoons (10 g) grated Parmesan cheese

Toss potatoes, onion, salt, basil and pepper in a mixing bowl. Arrange half of potato mixture in greased 11 × 7 × 2-inch (28 × 17¾ × 5 cm) baking dish. Sprinkle with half of the Swiss cheese. Pour tomato juice over the top; sprinkle with Parmesan cheese. Bake at 425°F (220°C) for 30 minutes or until potatoes are tender and top is golden brown. Makes six servings.

Artichokes in Garlic Broth

Preparation time: 9 minutes
Cooking time: 33 to 35 minutes

2 large or 4 medium artichokes
  Boiling water
3 tablespoons (45 *ml*) lemon juice
1 tablespoon (15 *g*) grated lemon peel
1 cup (250 *ml*) chicken broth

3 tablespoons (25 *g*) chopped parsley
2 tablespoons (30 *ml*) olive oil
3 cloves minced garlic
1 pinch coarsely ground pepper
  Salt

Pull off lower, outer petals of artichokes. Cut off top third of artichokes. Snip off tips of remaining petals. Cut stems to one inch (2 *cm*) or less. Stand artichokes in pot with three inches (8 *cm*) of boiling water; add lemon juice and peel. Cover and boil gently 10 minutes; remove and drain. Place in deep baking dish. Combine broth, parsley, oil, garlic, pepper and salt to taste; pour over artichokes. Bake,* covered, at 400°F (200°C) for 20 minutes or until petal near the center pulls out easily. Serve artichokes and liquid in soup dishes or bowls as an appetizer or vegetable side dish. Makes about four servings. Recipe can be halved.

Range-top method: Increase broth to 1⅓ to 1½ cups (325 ml to 375 *ml*) and olive oil to 3 tablespoons (45 *ml*). Simmer, covered, 20 minutes or until petal near the center pulls out easily.

Tip: Serve with warm sour dough bread to dip up juices. Serve as a main dish with cheese and bread. May also be served chilled.

Pasta Salad and Tangy Dressing

Preparation time: 10 minutes
Cooking time: 12 minutes

1 pound (450 *g*) spinach, stems removed, washed and
    drained
½ pound (225 *g*) bowtie pasta, cooked and drained
    Tangy Dressing
2 medium tomatoes, cut into small chunks
¼ pound (30 *g*) Monterey Jack (Double Gloucester) or
    Feta cheese, cubed
1 cup (125 *g*) pitted black olives, halved
2 tablespoons (30 *g*) chopped parsley
    Orange slices

Line a large salad bowl with a few spinach leaves.
Coarsely shred remaining leaves and toss with cooled
pasta and ½ cup (120 *ml*) *Tangy Dressing*. Pile in the salad
bowl. Arrange tomatoes, cheese cubes and olives in con-
centric circles on top. Sprinkle top with parsley and
garnish with orange slices. Pass remaining dressing.
Makes four to six servings.

Tangy Dressing

6 tablespoons (90 *ml*) red wine vinegar
½ cup (120 *ml*) vegetable oil
¼ cup (250 *g*) sugar
½ teaspoon (2 *g*) salt
¼ teaspoon (1 *g*) *each* thyme, rosemary, marjoram
    and pepper
1 medium clove garlic, minced

Combine all ingredients in a jar and shake well.

Honey Vinaigrette Salad Dressing
(not pictured)

⅓ cup (75 *ml*) red wine vinegar
¼ cup (75 *g*) honey
¼ cup (60 *g*) olive oil
2 tablespoons (30 *ml*) lemon juice
1½ teaspoons (7 *g*) dry mustard
    Salt and pepper to taste

Combine all ingredients; mix thoroughly. Serve over
fruit or vegetable salad. Makes 1¼ cups (250 *ml*).

Tip: By measuring the oil first, the honey will slide out of
the measuring cup.

Variation: Three-fourths to 1 teaspoon (3 to 5 *ml*) dried
basil, crushed, may be added.

Spinach Wok Salad

Preparation time: 8 minutes
Cooking time: 5 minutes

1 bunch spinach, washed
3 tablespoons (45 *ml*) oil
1 tablespoon (15 *ml*) vinegar
2 teaspoons (5 *g*) Dijon mustard
2 cloves garlic, minced
  Salt and pepper, to taste
1 bunch scallions (spring onions), cut in 2-inch pieces
2 carrots, thinly sliced
1 tomato, cut in wedges
1 cup (125 *g*) pitted ripe olives, whole or halved
1 avocado, sliced
½ cup (50 *g*) walnut pieces

Remove spinach stems; tear into bite-size pieces. Combine oil, vinegar, mustard, garlic, salt and pepper in electric wok. Heat at 325°F (160°C) two minutes. Add scallions and carrots; stir-fry one minute. Add remaining ingredients; stir-fry 30 seconds more. Cover; turn wok off. Serve from wok. Makes four servings.

Note: May be prepared in frying pan using medium high heat.

Index